CHRIST

The West Call him Jesus

By
Deborah Brown

AuthorHouse™
1663 Liberty Drive
Bloomington, IN 47403
www.authorhouse.com
Phone: 833-262-8899

ISBN: 978-1-6655-4053-7 (sc)
ISBN: 978-1-6655-4052-0 (e)

Print information available on the last page.

Published by AuthorHouse 02/21/2022

authorHOUSE

Scriptures From

NIV
KJV

Christ was replaced for Jesus in this book.
Christ means savior.

A Christian Chidren's Book. For ages 6-12. Bible verses are from NIV Bible and Lord's Prayer from KJV Bible.

Acknowledgement

Mother Lucille Whidby
My mother always believed in me.

Dedicated
To
My GrandChildren

Isaiah
Nile
Nia

CONTENTS

GOD'S NAME
Is
YAWEH
He created heaven
And Earth
He sent his son to
SAVE
The WORLD

His NAME
Is
Yehoshua

He is the son
Of
GOD

The Christ

Yehoshua
Yehoshua was born in the
Middle East. In the town
Of Bethlehem. He is Hebrew.

Yehoshua's
Earthly parents:
His father's and mother's Hebrew Names
are Yosef and Myriam.
Their Western Names are
Joseph and Mary

The Hebrews Call
GoD Yahweh

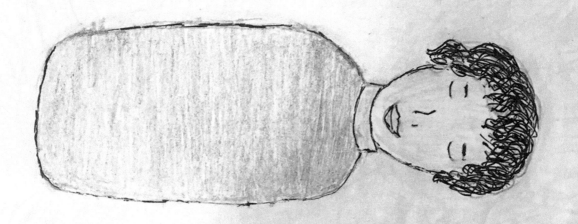

Luke 2: 8 — 14

Luke 2:8-14 NIV

⁸ And there were shepherds living out in the fields nearby, keeping watch over their flocks at night. ⁹ An angel of the Lord appeared to them, and the glory of the Lord shone around them, and they were terrified. ¹⁰ But the angel said to them, "Do not be afraid. I bring you good news that will cause great joy for all the people. ¹¹ Today in the town of David a Savior has been born to you; he is the Messiah, the Lord. ¹² This will be a sign to you: You will find a baby wrapped in cloths and lying in a manger."

¹³ Suddenly a great company of the heavenly host appeared with the angel, praising God and saying,

¹⁴ "Glory to God in the highest heaven, and on earth peace to those on whom his favor rests."

Psalm 121:1-2 NIV

¹ I lift up my eyes to the mountains—
where does my help come from?

² My help comes from the Lord,
the Maker of heaven and earth.

Proverb 3:5-6

[5] Trust in the LORD WITH ALL YOUR HEART
and lean not on your own understanding;
[6] in all your ways submit to him,
and he will make your paths straight.

Proverb 22:6

[6] Start children off on the way they should go,
and even when they are old they will not turn from it.

Joshua 24:15

¹⁵ But if serving the LORD seems undesirable to you, then choose for yourselves this day whom you will serve, whether the gods your ancestors served beyond the Euphrates, or the gods of the Amorites, in whose land you are living. But as for me and my household, we will serve the LORD."

Isaiah 55:6 NIV

⁶Seek the Lord while he may be found;
call on him while he is near.

Matthew 6:33 NIV

33 But seek first his kingdom and his righteousness, and all these things will be given to you as well.

Matthew 5:9 NIV

Blessed are the peacemakers,
for they will be called children of God.

Hebrew 11:1 NIV

11 Now faith is confidence in what we hope for and assurance about what we do not see.

Psalm 7:17 NIV

I will give thanks to the Lord because of his
righteousness;
I will sing the praises of the name
of the Lord Most High.

Job 5:17 NIV

[17] "Blessed is the one whom God corrects;
so do not despise the discipline of the Almighty.

Ecclesiastes 3:1

Ecclesiastes 3:1 NIV

3 There is a time for everything,
and a season for every activity under the heavens:

23 Psalm

¹ The Lord is my shepherd, I lack nothing.
² He makes me lie down in green pastures, he leads me beside quiet waters,
³ he refreshes my soul. He guides me along the right paths for his name's sake.
⁴ Even though I walk
through the darkest valley,[a]
I will fear no evil,
for you are with me;
your rod and your staff,
they comfort me.
⁵ You prepare a table before me
in the presence of my enemies.
You anoint my head with oil;
my cup overflows.
⁶ Surely your goodness and love will follow me
all the days of my life,
and I will dwell in the house of the LORD
forever.

1 Peter 5:6-9 NIV

⁶ Humble yourselves, therefore, under God's mighty hand, that he may lift you up in due time.
⁷ Cast all your anxiety on him because he cares for you.
⁸ Be alert and of sober mind. Your enemy the devil prowls around like a roaring lion looking for someone to devour. **⁹** Resist him, standing firm in the faith, because you know that the family of believers throughout the world is undergoing the same kind of sufferings.

Proverb 11:1 NIV

[11] The Lord detests dishonest scales,
but accurate weights find favor with him.

Acts 2:17-18 NIV

¹⁷ "'In the last days, God says,
I will pour out my Spirit on all people.
Your sons and daughters will prophesy,
your young men will see visions,
your old men will dream dreams.
¹⁸ Even on my servants, both men and women,
I will pour out my Spirit in those days,
and they will prophesy.

2 Corinthians 5:17 NIV

[17] Therefore, if anyone is in Christ, the new creation has come: The old has gone, the new is here!

Proverbs 24:16 NIV

16 for though the righteous fall seven times, they rise again, but the wicked stumble when calamity strike

MatthewS 7:5- 20

Matthews 7:5-20 NIV

⁵ You hypocrite, first take the plank out of your own eye, and then you will see clearly to remove the speck from your brother's eye.

⁶ "Do not give dogs what is sacred; do not throw your pearls to pigs. If you do, they may trample them under their feet, and turn and tear you to pieces.

⁷ "Ask and it will be given to you; seek and you will find; knock and the door will be opened to you.

⁸ For everyone who asks receives; the one who seeks finds; and to the one who knocks, the door will be opened.

⁹ "Which of you, if your son asks for bread, will give him a stone?

¹⁰ Or if he asks for a fish, will give him a snake?

¹¹ If you, then, though you are evil, know how to give good gifts to your children, how much more will your Father in heaven give good gifts to those who ask him!

¹² So in everything, do to others what you would have them do to you, for this sums up the Law and the Prophets.

¹³ "Enter through the narrow gate. For wide is the gate and broad is the road that leads to destruction, and many enter through it.

¹⁴ But small is the gate and narrow the road that leads to life, and only a few find it.

¹⁵ "Watch out for false prophets. They come to you in sheep's clothing, but inwardly they are ferocious wolves.

¹⁶ By their fruit you will recognize them. Do people pick grapes from thornbushes, or figs from thistles?

¹⁷ Likewise, every good tree bears good fruit, but a bad tree bears bad fruit.

¹⁸ A good tree cannot bear bad fruit, and a bad tree cannot bear good fruit.

¹⁹ Every tree that does not bear good fruit is cut down and thrown into the fire.

²⁰ Thus, by their fruit you will recognize them.

Mark 1:35 NIV

35 Very early in the morning, while it was still dark, Christ got up, left the house and went off to a solitary place, where he prayed.

1 Timothy 5:8 NIV

8 Anyone who does not provide for their relatives, and especially for their own household, has denied the faith and is worse than an unbeliever.

James 1:4

4 Let perseverance finish its work so that you may be mature and complete, not lacking anything.

Matthew 18:1-4 NIV

18 At that time the disciples came to Christ and asked, "Who, then, is the greatest in the kingdom of heaven?"

2 He called a little child to him, and placed the child among them. **3** And he said: "Truly I tell you, unless you change and become like little children, you will never enter the kingdom of heaven. **4** Therefore, whoever takes the lowly position of this child is the greatest in the kingdom of heaven.

Matthew 7:24-25 NIV

24 "Therefore everyone who hears these words of mine and puts them into practice is like a wise man who built his house on the rock. 25 The rain came down, the streams rose, and the winds blew and beat against that house; yet it did not fall, because it had its foundation on the rock.

Ecclesiastes 12: 1-2 NIV

¹² Remember your Creator
in the days of your youth,
before the days of trouble come
and the years approach when you will say,
"I find no pleasure in them"—
² before the sun and the light
and the moon and the stars grow dark,
and the clouds return after the rain;

Matthew 9:12-13 NIV

[12] On hearing this, Christ said, "It is not the healthy who need a doctor, but the sick. [13] But go and learn what this means: 'I desire mercy, not sacrifice.'[a] For I have not come to call the righteous, but sinners."

1 Peter 1:13-16 NIV

¹³ Therefore, with minds that are alert and fully sober, set your hope on the grace to be brought to you when Christ is revealed at his coming. **¹⁴** As obedient children, do not conform to the evil desires you had when you lived in ignorance. **¹⁵** But just as he who called you is holy, so be holy in all you do; **¹⁶** for it is written: "Be holy, because I am holy."

Proverbs 15:1-4 NIV

A gentle answer turns away wrath,
but a harsh word stirs up anger.
² The tongue of the wise adorns knowledge,
but the mouth of the fool gushes folly.
³ The eyes of the LORD ARE EVERYWHERE,
keeping watch on the wicked and the good.
⁴ The soothing tongue is a tree of life,
but a perverse tongue crushes the spirit.

Ephesians 3:14-18 NIV

¹⁴ For this reason I kneel before the Father, **¹⁵** from whom every family[a] in heaven and on earth derives its name. **¹⁶** I pray that out of his glorious riches he may strengthen you with power through his Spirit in your inner being, **¹⁷** so that Christ may dwell in your hearts through faith. And I pray that you, being rooted and established in love, **¹⁸** may have power, together with all the Lord's holy people, to grasp how wide and long and high and deep is the love of Christ,

John 14:1-4

14 "Do not let your hearts be troubled. You believe in God[a]; believe also in me. ² My Father's house has many rooms; if that were not so, would I have told you that I am going there to prepare a place for you? ³ And if I go and prepare a place for you, I will come back and take you to be with me that you also may be where I am. ⁴ You know the way to the place where I am going."

CHRIST

JOHN 14: 1-4

Matthew 6:9-13 KJV

⁹ After this manner therefore pray ye: Our Father which art in heaven, Hallowed be thy name.

¹⁰ Thy kingdom come, Thy will be done in earth, as it is in heaven.

¹¹ Give us this day our daily bread.

¹² And forgive us our debts, as we forgive our debtors.

¹³ And lead us not into temptation, but deliver us from evil: For thine is the kingdom, and the power, and the glory, forever. Amen.

The Lord's Prayer

Printed in the United States
by Baker & Taylor Publisher Services